Scott has been a poet and performer since the turn of the century. An award-winning comedian, creative director and multiple slam-winning poet (including the BBC Slam and UK Anti-Slam), he has performed his work at Glastonbury, the Edinburgh Fringe, the Prague Fringe, Kendal Calling, WOMAD, Larmer Tree and the Cheltenham Literature Festival. He has written for TV, radio and performed for Radio 4, Radio 3's the Verb, Sky Atlantic, ITV, BBC4 and BBC Arts. He lives in Newcastle with his wife, son, a goldfish, a one-eyed cat and a small fluffy dog.

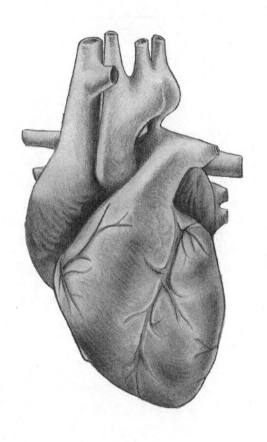

SCOTT TYRRELL

HONEST

Burning Eye

BurningEyeBooks
Never Knowingly
Mainstream

This edition published by Burning Eye Books 2018

www.burningeye.co.uk

@burningeyebooks

Burning Eye Books
15 West Hill, Portishead, BS20 6LG

ISBN 978-1-911570-45-5

Printed & bound by ImprintDigital.com, UK

'I do not like that man. I must get to know him better.'
Abraham Lincoln

For Margaret and Kenneth
who let me live

CHECKING THE REAR-VIEW MIRROR

The cliché has wheels. The sound of middle-age pulling up outside stops you in your tracks and dismantles you for frank examination. It is an intellectually innocent process in the driving seat, but under the bonnet the chassis and engine are being kicked, tinkered with and torn apart. I realise I'm a white male using car metaphors to talk about a mid-life crisis, but in truth fast or expensive cars were never my thing. Family is my thing. Work is my thing. Acknowledgement of good work is my fuel (*fuel* – there I go again).

When you reach the supposed mid-marker you want to look back and see you've achieved a bunch of stuff that paints you as a capable, intelligent and loved human being. In truth, despite some catastrophic false starts and engine misfires (I can't help myself now), I hadn't done too badly on paper for a working-class lad from an average start in South Shields. A brief diagnostic revealed a marriage to someone I still adore, two utterly non-boring kids, pets, a mortgage, a credible career in the creative industries and a side career as a poet and (sometimes) comic. But there were problems.

Over the last five years my wife's health had deteriorated and during a couple of major incidents had become life-threatening. There was an intense period when she was repeatedly in and out of hospital which weighed hard on us all. My son at this time was turning from a baby into a boy and inventing his personality whilst testing his and our boundaries. My stepdaughter was becoming a woman via archetypal teenage non-communication and I was slowly realising the real weight and pressure of parenting. To add to this, the environment at work was becoming toxic due to aggravating personalities. Then one day at my desk I couldn't think of an idea for a project. This was a first for me. Despite a personal history of crumbling walls and red finances I'd always been able to get something creative out of my head. But nothing I did this time budged creatively. At the end of the week I locked myself in the loo and I cried. I couldn't stop crying for a long time. The chassis had crumbled.

The bolts, tape and paint I'd patched on at dangerous

times in my life were now slowly dissolving in the wake of new duties, environments and responsibilities, revealing old, unchecked damage. I'd crammed so much away in compartments and pockets over the years and now it was all spilling out onto the seats and the floor.

I couldn't even begin tidying because every picture and scrap of memory I picked up was just too visceral. I was metaphorically sat in a broken-down car, surrounded by stubbornly ignored diaries and old photos and incapable of sorting any of them whilst being acutely aware that people were relying on me to be not broken.

This situation is not uncommon in the new millennium. We are all taking on far more than our minds and time can keep up with, and the norm is to be constantly and instantly connected with everyone else via social media. As such we are overwhelmed by every plight and opinion flashing at us in feeds and messages. We judge ourselves by the standards of others we respect (or those who seem to get more respect than we do). Everyone has become highly adept at self-marketing, and we see only the best projected version of everyone and naturally feel inferior to it. When masks slip, we feel betrayed or unsteady, or even smug when it's someone else's mask. None of this is healthy for a mind that wishes to walk confidently, earnestly and harmoniously with others. To compound it all, we find ourselves dancing on the most mentally unhealthy, divisive world political stage in decades. Cameron robbed the poor with austerity, the nationalistic have robbed the future with Brexit, and Trump has robbed the world of its peace of mind by being, well, Trump. All of the above is being added to the usual problems of everyday life with its lack of liberties, its hardships and its uncertainties. It is no wonder the sales of antidepressants are so healthy.

I found help for my particular situation, medically, psychologically, socially and familiarly. It has been a slow process to coolly and honestly pick apart the wreckage and build new foundations within me, but I am privileged to have had such warmth, humour and steel around me while I worked.

This book is an open examination of the weight that broke a poet's back, the people and personalities that propped me up and spun me around and the inherent optimism that exists in the core of most of us.

The process of writing revealed to me the ballast I still can't let go of, the surreal joy that skips around me daily and the light that refuses to go out. The engine in me still purrs. There are misfires, but there's petrol in the tank, plenty of mileage left and I can still find streets no one has driven on before. There's battered, vintage leather on the seats and some decent eclectic tracks blaring out of the speakers. The bodywork isn't flashy but the sparkplugs fire, the pistons work, the satnav is engaging and I can drive to some pretty interesting places.

Get in, if you like.[1]

---

[1] Sorry, the car metaphors spun way out of control.

CONTENTS

IF WE'RE BEING HONEST

If we're being honest
I'm broken in the places I didn't expect,
strong in places I rarely visit,
more thorough than my cavalier demeanour
would have you believe
and more wounded by
being ignored than insulted.

If we're being honest
I eat more ice cream whilst spooning it into the bowl
than what actually goes into the bowl.
I pee in the shower,
find pooing strangely erotic
and throw my clipped toenails behind the telly.

If we're being honest
I drink more than I used to,
run less than I used to,
weigh more than I used to
and masturbate at a consistent level
and sometimes when pets can see me.

If we're being honest
I respect cats more than dogs
because cats tend to leave the room
if they see me masturbating.

If we're being honest
I don't like much poetry
because some of it is tedious
thinly-veiled self-aggrandising
and some of it is better than
my ignorance can tell
and reading mine often reveals
all too painfully which camp it belongs,

which, if the former,
I pretend overlaps with the latter.
And if we're being really honest
some of it isn't actually poetry
but I'm hoping you won't be able to tell.

If we're being honest
putting spoken word
in a book makes as much sense
as buying a printed screenplay
or listening to a tour
of an art gallery on the radio.

If we're being honest
things aren't always political
and sometimes people just want to
get through the day
without joining any dots.

If we're being honest
the left is far more cunning at
truth selection than the right
because we care deeply about
the right not being right.

If we're being honest
most monsters are just people
stuck in a temporary swamp,
not strong enough yet to take
the hand more people
should be holding out.

If we're being honest
I hated my mother for twenty years
until I saw her be a grandmother,
then I hated myself for not seeing
the wood of grace and patience
for the trees of resentment.

If we're being honest
I'm not honest enough to be fully honest
because the accidental cup of lies
I spilled on the mountaintop of youth
is now an immovable glacier
in the valley of middle-age.

If we're being honest
I'm shit at metaphors.

If we're being honest
most religion doesn't hurt despite its dishonesty
and atheism doesn't hurt those who prefer dishonesty
and passive-aggressiveness isn't charming.

If we're being honest
in truth or dare I'll always tell the truth
because the truth behind me is easier to cope with
than the coercion in front.

If we're being honest
the phrase 'if we're being honest'
is a brutal preamble.
The cliff before the tempest.
The creaking door opening on a winter's night.
The harsh light on the operating table.
The slow sit down with hands clasped.

'If we're being honest'
invokes a cold intake of breath
because if we're being honest
it precedes words we can rarely take back.

But if we're being honest
we shouldn't need to.

HOOKED ON WORDS

Commissioned by BBC Radio 3 for the programme The Verb *at the Free Thinking Festival. The programme focussed on national and regional identity.*

'Scrap! Scrap! Scrap!'
The words rang like a fire alarm
as I felt the back of my head vibrate like a tuning fork.
'Come on then!' yelled his livid crumpled face,
his cheeks and temple as red
as the stripes on his shirt.
'Come on!'
As the mob gathered like moths to his flame
I had no time to wonder why
I was fending off his blows and spit
until I heard an explanation from the crowd.
'He hates Mackems! Smack 'im, man!'
Two minutes later a teacher
had both our ears in his nip.
'He started it!' yelled my assailant.
'He dissed Sunderland!'
'I just said I didn't like football,' I pleaded.
The teacher was disappointed in both of us.
He supported the Toon.

My childhood was often this confusing.
Life was a web of tripwires
revealing assumed allegiances.
We were pilots trying to glide
within the airspace of acceptable nuance,
playing hopscotch to avoid being too posh,
too articulate, too up ourselves,
lest we be compared to Sting.

To our chagrin the country painted us all as Geordies.
But we were Sand Dancers, Mackems, Monkey Hangers,
Smoggies, Pit Yackers, Magpies,
Black Cats and the Boro.
Tiny Venn diagrams that dared not overlap in public.

Fierce white tribes with barely a swatch of colour
protruding from the sleeves of our footie shirts.

Recipes were made from the
collective pantry of linguistics.
We were Radgie Gadgies and Workie Tickets,
canny hinnies and moanin' Minnies.
It was mint, lush and positively belter
to have a proper plodge in the lexicon clarts.
We were fierce poets who dared not admit
our love of language,
word wizards denying our trade,
but even pronunciation was fiercely fought.

It's NewCASTLE, not NEWcastle.
It's 'artlepool, not Hartlepool.
It's the Stadium of Light, not the Stadium of Sh…
…ared land and shared words
expertly carved up by the Lilliputians of the North East.

I once nearly saw a fight break out
over the correct pronunciation of
William Shatner's seminal cop show *TJ Hooker*.

It's Hoohkah!
It's Hewkuh!
It's 'ewker!

But we all agreed the show was crap.

We battled in the margins,
raged against the irrelevant,
all the while knowing names were no substitute
for the people behind them,
knowing that people mattered more
than the words that bound them.

For most of us.
But some get hooked on words.
Some let the sharp edge gouge their cheeks

and pull at their patience.
Some swallow the bitter brine of words
and let themselves be caught out of water,
dangling and desperate,
exhausted from the weight of hate,
clenched teeth and beaten brow,
someone else's catch now.

And thou shall be a fishy on a little dishy.
Thou shall be a net full of the most forgetful
folk who see disorders just because of borders,
loving just their colours, hating all the others,
shutting doors in faces of folk from strange places.

This is a big sea
and we're free to swim in any school that lets us thrive.
There are nets and hooks waiting,
cunning and subtle and telling us they're on our side,
but there really isn't a side to be on.
And we can swim fast or slow or as weirdly as we like.
All the bonny fish.

And our names will do no harm
and our words will break no skin
and our will shall be to disarm
and we'll see only kith and kin
and our spirit will not be sold
and our world will not be bleak
and the hooks will not take hold
if we just keep our tongue in our cheek.

THE MOUNTAIN

My stomach twisting and my throat
retching, I prick up my ears
to hear a junior doctor starting his shift.
His crackling, cocky enthusiasm
pervades through the ward
like a hand buzzer.
A nurse is reeling off the patients to him.
'And there's a kid who's taken an overdose.
He's in cubicle two.'
He tuts. 'Girlfriend left him, has she?'
I crack a smile, the vomit and sticky spit
still dripping down my chin.

Girlfriend.
Doing this because of a girlfriend.
Wouldn't that be so easy?
So normal?
So conventional?
I could get behind the romance of that,
the beautiful simplicity of it.
I fall in love for a moment with that
alternative reality.
But there is no girlfriend.
Just pain
and a hatred of this lump that I stall
and splutter around in
and the 'friends' who used me as the punching runt
and the mother drowning her heartache in wine
and the bad, angry man she clings to
soaked in cheap sherry
and the father and his new wife
who despises this slug I have become.

They wait outside, silently blaming each other.
I recognise that this is the new bottom
and there is some strange peace in that.
That I have landed.

After months of planning and resolve
I did it and then chickened out because
my heart was beating so fast in my chest
I thought I was going to explode rather than slip away.
Because of one tiny bastard light in my brain that said
We're not done yet.

I survey the bottom of this well and take stock.
What have we got that's good?
Some flair.
Some skills.
A sense of humour even in this toilet.
And there's the mountain up there,
and it's a big one.
I might not have enough
but I've got more than nothing.

I wipe the detritus from my mouth,
find my feet and slowly straighten up.
I'm immediately sick again in the bucket.
I wipe, straighten up again,
control the nausea and find
part of a start in my head.
A list is writing itself.
Just a small one.
Baby steps.
I resolve to check off the first item.
I pull back the curtains and look
at their broken, confused faces.
'I'm OK,' I say. 'I guess we need to talk.'

A LETTER TO IDENTITY

There are those who knew you back then.
The ink in your shadow made it into
the chapters in their head.
Every line a collaboration,
written for better or worse.
All printed and bound.

But that was then.
A different 'you'.
The 'you' you kicked against.
The half-heartedly written 'you' with all the
embarrassing notes in the margins
and the messy circular story
that wouldn't end.
The 'you' you wished would just pick a plotline.

But you are the editor-in-chief now.
Extensive rewrites and many book cover designs later,
your prose is clean and your story is going somewhere.
You're proofed and print-ready.

But those chapters you penned back then,
all those sketchy riffs and plotless cul-de-sacs,
all the incidental walk-ons
that never reached a conclusion,
they still exist in other people's books,
informing all manner of adventures taken.

All the clangers you dropped
and silences that lingered,
all those ticks, smiles and beaten brows,
the experimental clothes and paint worn,
the tunes and thoughts that sneaked out,
the involuntary chuckles and tears,
the kindness in spite of yourself,
the hours so dark it's hard to remember
anything but blots and smudges,

the moments you never footnoted,
the nuance you never saw in a mirror,
the honesty you never knew you spoke,
all sit in those pages casting shadows,
turning cogs, steering paths.

And you can't destroy those pages
and you can't pretend they don't exist
and you shouldn't be afraid of them.
You made them.
The honest, struggling, broken 'you'.
You wrote every line
and you can't rewrite them.
You can only give them new meaning.

So add to them.
Make and sell that new, better testament
but don't forget the old one.
It's there to read in so many copies
and some pages are loved dearly
by those who read between the lines.

THOSE WOMEN

Grrr.
They pushed me, those women.
They said I was lazy, them women.
They made my do things all by myself.
They made me shut up with their
you've-said-enoughness.
They made me listen to their
think-before-you-speakness.
They confused me with their
it's-up-to-youness.
They clarified things with their
it's-not-happening-till-you-do-thisness.
They said I could do better with their
are-you-leaving-it-like-thatness.
They made me do better with their
you'll-stay-there-till-it's-doneness.
They told me I did better with their
there's-still-room-for-improvementness.
They let me in with their kindness.
They let me further in with their you-and-meness.
They let me stay with them, those women.
They made the world smell and taste good
without cooking a thing.
They made me work for the taste.
They made me ask nicely for the smells.
They made me feel better for that.
They made me feel closer for that.
They made me feel.
They made me.

BLUE BADGE OF HONOUR

You probably don't see it,
that there's anything wrong.
With the eyes of a bush baby
and a smile that can make you
forget what you came for,
she puts you at such ease.

She has a blue badge; she's very lucky.
Motorists watch us park with envy.
It takes a while for them to notice
the ever-so-subtle difference in her walk.
Hardly anything wrong at all.

She has a family.
She works full-time.
She does what she can.
It's hard for anyone.

She isn't anyone.
She was born with too small a spinal column
clinging tight to the tail of her brain,
exposed by a gape at the base of her back
and a left leg that would never catch up to her right.
They patched her up with seventies science
and told her mother not to expect too much.
Underestimating her, like so many to come.

She taught herself to ignore the insults
from the type of idiot she now teaches English to.
She lights fires under the mattresses
of their indifference.
They like her
and the cunning she hides behind the smile.

Behind the smile it's battle stations
as every movement grates and crunches within her.
She heaves hard as an athlete

just to stand still, to walk without grimace,
her body bearing the scars of myriad operations,
of trials and bad ideas and last resorts,
of life-threatening prodding and poking
and buck-passing and hand-washing
and shrugs and drugs.
Her throat an apothecary's abyss.

She sees us move with alien eyes,
watching the world float about with breathtaking ease,
our muscles and bones
never questioning their journeys,
flabby and indulgent in their ocean of choice,
while she creaks and cracks and jars and sears,
forcing such economy of movement as to make her act
with pure purpose and enviable grace.
She has such grace

and strength.
I am a feather to her fortress.
If she falls, it is she that will hold me up.
It is she that will save that day.
All I can do is try to be worthy of the time
she wants to spend with me.
To be worthy of a true hero
with a blue badge.

HIS BROKEN GODDESS

With cracked, classic chic
and warm, cobbled light
jostling through her ruined architecture,
she is his moveable altar.
He worships before her,
bringing offerings of art, food and stories.
He is her highest priest,
her cracked conduit,
an obsessed scatterbrain cleric
with bursts of pious devotion
erupting from his arms and lips.
She barely survives his adoration.
She wishes his zeal could be more
evenly distributed in this world
and her testaments better adhered to.
But she pins his drawings on the fridge all the same
and tells the world he is her word made flesh.

WORTH IT

Clumsy pudgy arms lasso bleary,
barely awake parents into
an uncomfortable family bouquet
as he pecks at both our cheeks
like an indecisive woodpecker

We're feeling the love.
Our cheeks and necks are red with it.
There were moments,
whole years in fact, not so long ago,
when I would weep in longing
for a feeling this big, this tidal.
When a stranger's touch
on the hairs on my arm
would force an intake of breath.

'Do you love your people?' I ask.
He continues to kiss us.
'What would you do if your parents weren't together?
Would that be awful?'
He stops, sits up and ponders.
'Who would be my real parent?'
'What do you mean?' I ask.
'Who would I stay with?'
'Well, I suppose we'd share you.'
He looks worried. That was a careless door to open.
'That's not going to happen, though!' chimes in his mum.
He relaxes.
Then the glee of the brand-new illuminates his face.

'Let's have a competition,' he shrieks,
'to see who I'll stay with!'
'We're not splitting up,' I remind him.
'I'll ask you each some questions,' he continues,
'and the winner gets to stay with me.'
'You're really running with this now, aren't you?' I sigh.
He clears his throat.

'Question one. What is Mum's favourite cake?'
'Chocolate!' squeaks his mum.
'Correct! Question two. If I was ice cream,
what flavour would I be?'
'Chocolate?' I suggest.
'No!'
'Tutti frutti!' says his mum.
'Yes! Well done!'
'You don't even know what tutti frutti is,' I complain.
'That's two to Mum. Next question…'
'I'm not going to win, am I?' I ask.
'Probably not.'
'Should I pack?'
'I think Mum would like a coffee first.'

WHAT'S IN A NAME?

I hear him stomping down the stairs
and he marches into the lounge
like a burning elephant.
'I hate my name!'
I down my book, sigh and resign myself
to the imminent, nonsensical freefall
down his oncoming rabbit hole.
'You have a lovely name,' argues his mum.
'It suits you.'
'Toby is a cute name. A child's name.
If I keep it I'll never be treated as an adult.'
'You're seven,' I remind him.
'I'm nearly eight.'
'So what name would you prefer?' asks his mum.
His face contorts as he stares at the wall.
He walks out the room for a moment,
muttering to himself,
then storms back in defiantly.
'Elmer.'

OUT TO LUNCH

Turning my coat collar down, I enter the lounge
to see him holding one sock,
his eyes glued to shrill colours
screaming out of a plasma screen.
'Aren't you ready yet? We're going to the Badger for lunch.'
He doesn't look up. 'What badger?'
'It's a place that serves food. We've been before.'
He locates the remote, mercifully finds the pause button
and stares up at me.
'The badger? We're not going inside a large badger?'
'We're not.'
'We won't be eaten by an enormous badger?'
'We won't be, no.'
'Because that would be the worst café ever.'
'Agreed.'
He takes a plastic sword just in case.

ADVANCED MATHEMATICS

'Right, I've got a difficult one,' I say.
'Bring it.'
'If a giant could wear a sock on his little finger,
how many Smarties could you fit up his nose?'
He's stumped. This one is a real poser even for him.
'I reckon… enough for all the people in England to have one each.'
'Close. It's France.'
'I always get the country wrong,' he humbly admits.
'Give me another. Yours are more fun than SPAG.'
'Ah, oui, and probably more accurate.'

BAD DAD

The innocent kaleidoscopic splay
of the John Lewis toy department
clashes awkwardly with the lustful chorus of
'Don't Let the Bells End'
as we shift and sigh in the queue.

Every few seconds he must be wrenched
from wriggling irritation with random
and increasingly desperate distractions.
'Count how many baubles you can see on that tree.'
'No. Can we get this?'
'No.'
'Is this supposed to come off?'
'Just put it back.'

There's a family in front,
all Cath Kidston, Mini Boden, polite smiles
and appropriate small talk.
They bask in the glow of being the perfect clientele.
They radiate cheer.
They smell of nutmeg
and I'm lost in a Waitrose fantasy of Nigella mince pies
and River Cottage nut roast
served in a snowed-in thatched cottage
lit with Yankee candles.

'Next!' yells the assistant.
I shuffle my awkward, tatty, tubby self forward,
offspring in tow.
The assistant, Debbie, smiles at him.
'These for you?'
'No.'
'Your dad not buying anything for you? Bad dad!'
'He hurt me.'

Debbie clutches.
I can feel it.

I see the smile leave her eyes.

'What do you mean, I hurt you?'
'I don't like it when you hurt me.'
'I never hurt you.'
'You hurt me in bed.'
'I never hurt you in bed!'
'You hurt me in bed this morning.'

'Good job social services aren't here,' quips Debbie.
'I've no idea what he's talking about.' I desperately chuckle.
And I don't.

But now
I'm *that* man.
The man who hides terrible things
and is finally lynched by the tongues of babes.
I am the most despicable there is.
Everything that's rotten.
I am the shameful tune played on dirty instruments.
I am the spider in the shadows,
the dark web.

Eyes chisel me into *Daily Mail* columns
as we file past the queue.
My son ambles in blind oblivion
to the terrorist bomb he just detonated
in a busy department store.

I am incandescent with this child.
I am burning at his betrayal,
fizzing,
foaming,
furious.
He is so going to…
I am so going to…
be his dad.

I take a knee. 'How did I hurt you?'
'Oh, you elbowed me when we were
watching *Labyrinth* on your bed.'

Bastard.

'Does it still hurt?'
'Not really. Can we get a muffin now?'
'Yes, we can get a muffin now.
But not in this shop.'

GABRIEL

We hear slow arrhythmic steps coming down the stairs.
The cogs in his mind are whirring,
throwing spanners at his motor skills.
There's a question somewhere in this plodding descent.
We brace ourselves for something the entire
Encyclopaedia Britannica doesn't have a page for.

'Dad, do you remember Gabriel? You spent the night
with him before you were in love with Mum?'
I slowly turn to my wife.
She has coffee dribbling out of her mouth
and is shaking like a dog's leg, mid-scratch.
'What are you talking about?' I ask.
'Who's Gabriel?'
'You told me! Before you met Mum.
You slept with Gabriel.'
'I have absolutely no idea what you mean.'
'Gabriel!' he asserts. 'Gabriel!
You shared a bed with him.'
My wife has slid off the sofa
and is actually squeaking now.
'I seriously don't… do you mean Adrian?' I ask.
'My best man at our wedding?'
'Maybe,' he says.
'We shared a house.'
'You slept in the same bed. You told me.'
'We may have slept in the same bed
if we were staying at someone else's house
or camping, maybe.'
'So you slept together?'
'We slept next to each other, sometimes.'
'So you had a good relationship, then?'

Probably the healthiest relationship
I've ever had with a man of my generation.
There was respect and understanding.
We took the time to articulate ideas

and concerns to each other
with intelligence and empathy.
We could talk in eyes and sighs.
We would set out to watch the sun rise on beaches,
battle through snow in clapped-out cars.
We would weep in each other's arms,
hold each other in pain and triumph
and the break would never be awkward.
Eyes would meet and our gaze would say
I know and I'm here.
I loved him as a brother and a mind
I had longed to connect with since
I was old enough to frame thoughts into words,
and I miss him very much.

But I don't say any of that.
I say, 'Yeah, we were mates'
and slide back under the quilt
of brittle masculinity as I walk out of the room
to avoid framing male love as something beautiful.

SNAPPING BACK

I'm fiddling with a plastic leg in a queue for popcorn.
'It just snaps back, Dad,'
advises my extraordinarily helpful son,
'but be gentle.'
'If you had been gentle in the first place
I wouldn't be doing this, and where's her shoe?
Find her shoe.'
He fans about the foyer, arms out, palms down
like they're Barbie shoe detectors
whilst I try to fit an easily breakable plastic bearing
into an easily breakable plastic cavity
because my easily distracted son
can't not get easily overexcited
watching a Disney trailer whilst gripping a doll.

I'm still fiddling when I realise
he's actually trying to fit the shoe back on to the foot
while the leg's still detached
and I'm torn between scolding his stupidity
and praising him for finding a tiny pink shoe
on a sprawling red carpet.
At that moment the leg snaps back in
and I can't help myself.
'Yes!' I exclaim at an uncomfortably high volume.
'Did it!' I hand it to him, but he doesn't take it.

'Here, have it.'
He frowns and flashes a look to my right,
turns his back and I know what's going on.
I shove the doll in my shoulder bag, turn around
and there they are.
A prepubescent pack of hyenas
in a sniggering circle,
shooting millisecond eyeballs at us.
We are the afternoon's unexpected entertainment.
We will be more discussed
than the film they're about to see.

We are the freak show, the weirdos,
the delicious new targets to bond over.

I'm cursing my son's oddness under my tongue,
scorning his orbiting of the pink and frilly,
blasting him in my mind for putting me in this position,
but I know none of this is helpful
as the responsibility to be his parent
overrides my embarrassment
and in that moment, I remember Sindy.

My sister's Sindy doll.
For two nights when I was six
she slept on my pillow and I adored her.
She made me feel excited and contented
because girls were Neverland to me.
Big eyes, tantalising smells,
magnetic smiles, soft voices,
handstands, cartwheels and secrets.
And I remember when Sindy
was discovered on my pillow.
The disappointed eye-rolling.
The pursed lips.
The derisory vicious tittering.
The scorched bone-deep embarrassment.

I put my hand on my son's shoulder.
My son who loves girls.
My son who plays with girls.
My son who respects girls.
'If you're worried about them, don't be,' I say.
'It's their problem, not yours. Take the doll.
Play with it. Be yourself. Just don't break the legs off again.'
'They should be stronger,' he says.
'You're right, they should be stronger.'

SUPERHEROES' LIB

Whilst picking up socks, small plastic handbags
and scrunched-up drawings
I notice the twelve-inch Batgirl
I bought him for his birthday.
She is redressed in Barbie jeans, stripy top,
pink heels and a backpack.
'She doesn't look much like Batgirl anymore,' I observe.
'She has a life outside of being Batgirl, you know.
You should let her wear what she wants.'
'I will,' I concede.
'And it's Barbara when she's not working.'

SHE DOESN'T KNOW

The conversations have become less
and the entrances are usually
via the doorway of popular culture,
but there's still depth to us.
I think she believes I've stopped caring.
That she has her life and we have ours,
her mother, her little brother and I,
and that there's little room in my head for her now.
She doesn't know that I'm still curious about
who she is and who she wants to be
because plans don't stop at twenty.

She doesn't know that I vividly remember
how it feels to be confused and out of place.
To have so much new grownuppery to sort
and no boxes to put it in.
How exhausting it is to care
about everything but yourself
and how easy it is to slip
into being the person you think they want
rather than letting them see the you
you're fixing for yourself
and celebrating that.

She doesn't know I believe that
Hermione Granger was the real hero
and that most of the arguments we had
were to challenge preconceptions
because her intellect can take it
and because that's what Hermione would do
and Lyra.

She doesn't know how glorious it was for me to
see her so invested in the written and spoken word
when we read to each other over those evenings, long ago.
How powerful it was to see her visibly shake with rage
when they tried to cut Pantalaimon away

and how she wept at the end of *Mice and Men*.
Tell me about the rabbits, George.

She doesn't know that I have so much
faith in her finding her truest path
and that I trust her to work all of this out
and that I'm here to be wherever she needs someone to be
before anyone else can get there,

or maybe she does.
She is pretty smart.

THE RIGHT DREAMS

In some snug, twilight hinterland
they wrap themselves in their warm quilts
and sleepwalk through liberated streets
strewn with red and white flags and white faces
beaming with relief, pride and the ruddy hue
of English bitter's gentle bruising.

Cigar smoke billows from pub windows
to the sound of 'God Save the Queen'
(the original version)
sung by patriots whose jobs weren't stolen.

They shuffle past the unemployed,
gleefully cashing their giros,
secure in knowing only English jobseekers
will feed themselves with these.

They amble through village fêtes and past chapels
where overly excited vicars iron vestments
and dust off Bibles to read with newfound zealotry,
their competition in tatters.

Through quiet cities humming with familiar accents
in streets where people are called Bill and Mary
and an honest Tommy courts an English Rose
and goes off to fight Middle Easterners
in the name of a 2,000-year-old Middle Easterner.

Tiptoeing past secure old cottages
guarded by righteous trigger-fingers
and up into rolling hills
strewn with the carcasses of wind turbines
to where the English lion lies down
with the English lamb and finally
there is honest, reserved, God-fearing, English peace.

Peace at last.

But for the foghorn of creativity and innovation
ebbing into a slow march of stultifying predictability
as the battleground for ideas and culture
that forge history whispers away to fragility and dust.
And for the whimpers of the quietly terrified
waving goodbye to lovers and friends on bulging vessels to
some corner of a foreign field that is forever England.

The real England.
The great patchwork quilt
stitched with threads spun
from every corner of the Earth.
The England with all the fabrics of the ages
brightening and warming its cold mattress.
That beautiful, warm, hotchpotch quilt
that stoic hands and open minds made.
Wake up and hold it tight around you.
You'll be cold when it's gone.

PRAYER FOR THE SELFISH

Blessed Conservatives,
our fair-minded and privately educated overlords,
we beseech thee to overcome the foreign swarms
desperate to invade our shores for our precious benefits.
May you deny them the covetous bounty of £36.62 per week
as they slowly recover from seeing
their loved ones detonated.
May they be blinded by the radiant light
of your smug, self-satisfied grins
and so row away from this green and pleasant land
which is, after all, completely full up
(apart from the 98% that's not, but we need that bit
to chase foxes on once the ban's lifted).
Have the compassion to gather up these poor souls
into someone else's arms.
Try the Germans.
They owe us for ruining the twentieth century anyway.
We pray that these pitiful unfortunates may find a little piece
of someone else's hospitality,
for we have hungry mouths of our own to feed,
provided they are actively looking for work,
disabled people to encourage
by tipping them out of their wheelchairs
and homeless to house
because we just remembered they exist this week.
For we are thy servants.
Austerity be thy name
and Murdoch and Dacre be thy messengers.
Amen.

WHAT DO YOU TALK ABOUT?

So, when evening comes
and you stop reading the reports,
fielding the calls, pacifying perplexed interviewers
and scribbling your seal of approval
on the fates of millions,

when you switch off your office light
and your earnest solemn smile
and join buttoned-tight friends and colleagues
in ancient private rooms,

when you loosen the belt,
kick off those tight, mirror-polished shoes
and sink into a dark leather chair
croaking with the rasp of fierce wealth
and sip well-aged amber from fine crystal,

when you and your lieutenants
gather round a festooned historic tapestry
atop a magnificent stone fireplace
and you give those oh-so-subtle nods to each other
knowing you've made it,
at the top of the pile,
in an elite circle of confidence,
certain that no one will tell, backchat,
paraphrase or hold your words against you,
in or out of context,
assured you can say what the hell you like now,
absolutely anything at all,
what do you talk about?

Is it about whips and majorities and percentage polls
and the next steps to securing footholds in history?
Is it about congratulation, a few could-do-betters
and benign concerns about the best value
you could be giving the British public?
Would it be cheeky, knowing

Westminster banter,
snobbish but harmless,
alien and intriguing but honest and serving,
the way you would want us to hear it?

Do you laugh at the cock-ups of colleagues?
Amusing media appearances?
Parallels to satirical news shows?
Life imitating art?

Do you still pinch yourself
that you're in charge of it all?
Do you tell your confidantes as much?
And what do they tell you?
What do they say about how it's all going?
Do they mention us at all?
The 'us' who don't like how it's going?
How do we, the people,
fare in your private conversations,
in your private thoughts?
What do you really see in us?

Do you see the potential of an entire planet
simmering in a wonky island-shaped pot:
a tagine-wok-casserole-deep-fat-frying-cauldron
of human life?
A formidable force of cloudy,
collaborative, inclusive clout?
Or do you see tiny homes and tiny lives
and breathe a deep sigh of relief
that by good fortune and the grace of your god
you were afforded high enough walls
that the tiny people couldn't scale?
Do you feel assured that one's will and mind
are the only true adversities,
having had all the rest expensively
bulldozed from one's path?

Do you stand convinced that your status and wealth
bestow upon you a natural right
to be counted amongst the ruling class?
And does the fact that so many of us, the people,
buy into this archaic system gird you in this belief?
Or do you know deep down the absurdity of such a
money-fuelled power-hungry legacy but are so sewn in
to its fabric that all you can do is bow to its tenacity?

Or are you just laughing at us?
Are you all standing around that tapestry,
sipping from those tumblers,
having a good old guffaw
at the tiny people under your care?
Because that's how it feels.

And you may say I'm paranoid
and that it's all about the long term
and that I wouldn't understand
and that I should be grateful
for your vision of a prosperous Britain.
But I'm not.

And it's not because mine are on your hit list.
On paper, we slip smoothly into your big blue net.
We work full-time at higher-educated professions.
We have two kids and try damn hard
to be the parents they deserve.
We find time between us to make cushions and write poetry.
We holiday in this country.
You'd love us.
But here's what you don't get:
we don't think it should all be about us.
We are not the venal, scuttling,
grab-what-you-can vermin you take us for.
We actually do care about the rest.

I'd like to hold a vision of you all in that room
standing by that ancient tapestry
talking unguardedly about how hard it is to get it right,
your lieutenants unpolitically pouring out
their mistakes and their desires to make good,
determined, bone-determined to listen
to the front-liners and the strained and the pained
and with revelatory clarity
recognising that colossal, invisible
benefactor of privilege
and finally understanding
its awesome, destructive power,
and with raw, beautiful tears vowing
to be the public servants we all deserve.
To use whatever powers
they wield to fix and to heal
and to give to those who truly need it.

And you,
you'd smile and be sniff-proud
at how forthright your people are,
beaming that you'd chosen well in those
that would always do the right thing
even in the face of losing face.

And then you'd talk about family.
You'd tell self-deprecating, unguarded truths and stories.
You'd express honest concerns about those you love,
whether you're doing right by them,
and you'd unabashedly say
you'd do anything to keep them safe.
Just like the rest of us,
struggling to do the best we can
for those we cherish and wishing goodwill for the rest.

But then…
I hear faint chuckles and tiny titters

growing like the vines of a stinging nettle.
Spreading, sprawling up an ancient,
high, institutional wall
into austere, mocking, pitiless hysterics
echoing in that opulent hollow chamber.
And you stop and finish your drink and leave
to start another day.

ECHOES

Frightened and fragile and swimming in choice,
determined that everyone hears your voice,
neck-deep in thoughts bailed out with your phone,
assured of your ground, terrified you're alone.

Bandwagons jumped on and glued to groups
who flatter and like and never say 'oops'
when they get it wrong or skew the news
or mob-pick the zeitgeist to flash-mob abuse.

You're the warrior in the comfy seat,
context-free and incomplete,
living the life and lucid dream,
the unaccountable sovereign supreme.

Your views make you one of the people's heroes.
There's moral might in those ones and zeroes.
All the likes and shares mean you're never wrong,
every love and retweet chirping your song.

You've been posting for days
and your friends are responding,
opinions are bonding,
dissenters absconding.
Keep biting, keep writing,
keep corresponding.

Every clapping emoji props up your plight.
Every thumbs-up affirms you're right in your fight.
Every argument playing to current vexation,
relying on unconfirmed quotes and citation
and biased, edited, twisted filtration,
proving nothing but how to find self-vindication.

So sing in echoes if it helps you up
and gets you dressed and fills your cup.
Preach to the flocking sycophants

who'll back you up when you're talking pants.
Line up the traitors who've clashed and fought
and convict them in your kangaroo court.

Banish them all from virtual sight.
This world can only be black and white.
Dishcloth grey won't float your boat.
You're playing at home with the popular vote.
Don't let them in and change your mind
and question what you have enshrined.

Stay where it's cosy and folk agree
in a construct replete with bonhomie,
in a safe, self-satisfied dominion,
for the big wide world's just too full of opinion.

NOT FROM THE HEART

The heart is a muscle that pumps
blood round your body.
It's rubbish at making a choice.
As a life coach it tends
to be pretty shoddy,
architecturally split
from your voice.
It's unable to persuade you to follow your dreams
or tell you you've fallen in love.
Its ventricles are assuredly not receptacles
for emotional matters thereof.
So, if you pine or ache or yearn or long,
of the location do not be misled,
for when someone resolves
to break your heart
they're really breaking your head.

STAMP YOUR FEET, SON

Commissioned by 'Christmas at the Cathedral' in aid of the Bobby Robson Foundation.

On a cold Boxing Day afternoon
a father and son shuffle along a row
up the Gallowgate end
and take their place in the Toon platoon.
'Stamp your feet, son. Stamp out the cold.
You'll soon forget you're freezing when it kicks off.'
A ten-year-old boy does as he's told,
feeling silly at first, but his dad joins in,
then the grey-haired, wrapped-up man
to his right follows suit.
Then the rest of the row shows willing
and soon the giggles warm his cheeks
and he starts to feel part of it.

He tightens his pristine black and white scarf
and sniffs the newness.
Everything about this day is raw
and he can tell his dad is nervous.
First match with his boy, hoping it's not the last.

The war cries have already started,
an undulating sonic wave
barely decipherable to the untrained ear.
'What they singing, Dad?'
'It's better you don't know yet, son.'
'Mam said there'd be swearing.'
'What's said in St James' stays in St James'.'
Soon after the toss, white leather strikes white leather
and the battle and swearing begin.

Expert advice spat from plump cheeks
filled with overpriced pie
(which for the purposes of decency
will be replaced by bleeps)

administered furiously
to some of the finest sportsmen in the world
and it in turn stocks up the vocabulary
of a ten-year-old boy.

'Oi, Ref. Should have gone to bleeping Specsavers!'
'Bleeping bleep. Who taught you to bleeping pass? Stevie
bleeping Wonder?'
'Yes, you bleeping beauty! Make my bleeping year.'
'You utter bleep.'
'Bleep off, you bleeping bleeped-up bleeper – that was a
bleeping penalty, you bleeping bleep!'
'Aww, for bleep's sake.'

The boy soaks in this vast lake of feeling.
Waves of support and attack
fired like arrows across a floodlit pitch.
A battle raging on and over a patch of green.
A tug of war on a ball.
Tens of thousands willing and heaving
it between two nets.
The cold isn't felt anymore, just every moment
slowed and precise and calibrated.
No thought, just feeling.
Thousands of hawks playing
their own games of strategy,
trying to telepathically tell twenty-two men
where to run, where to stand, who to mark
and, if that doesn't work, screaming it at them.

The boy watches the man he came with
alive and on fire.
The light has now left the sky
and taken its place in his dad's eyes,
flashing hope and belief,
and every time they meet his son's
there is something new.

The boy is infected, converted,
euphoric and magnetised for ninety minutes
and then…

As the crowd of black and white shuffle out the
Gallowgate end like a mob of impatient zebras
a glum boy stares at his feet.
'What's up, kidda?'
'What's up? We didn't win.'
They stop by the corner of the Milburn stand
and his dad looks up at a bronze suited man
resting on a ball with his hands in his pockets,
looking south to the city.

'See him, see his face? Always makes me smile.
He was a talented bloke. Played to win. Wanted to win,
but that's not what he'll be remembered for.
Not what he'll be loved for. He was a trier.
A decent, honest trier. Can I ask you a question?'
'Aye,' says his son.
'Were you cold during the game?'
'Not really.'
'That's passion, lad. That's caring. That's belief.
Blocks out the cold and everything else,
and you could fill a thousand stadiums
with the belief he had. He didn't always win
but he never stopped believing he could,
and he never stopped believing in those
who believed it too, and he definitely
would have believed in you.'

His son hides an embarrassed smile in his scarf.
His dad catches the edges of it.
'So, do you fancy coming back here?
Give these overpaid idiots another chance?'
'Aye, alright. Can we get the Metro, Dad?
I'm freezin' now.'

The two walk on.
The bronze statue watches them disappear
into the hazy, sodium light of the city.

'Stamp your feet, son.
Stamp out the cold.
You'll soon forget you're freezing
when you come back.'

GRANDDAD'S GETAWAYS

He was freest behind the wheel.
Always taking the scenic routes
through single-track roads
lined with dry stone walls and ponies.
Washes of green, blue, gold and lavender
strobed by like pastoral star fields.

Through cobbled side streets
and passes skirting mountain lakes
he meandered and eased
through litters of lambs
and passels of pigs
and juddered over cattle grids.

They whipped by as he breathed in
memories and fantasies of
open spaces, sprawling sunsets and wild air
light years from urban myopia.

Time was relative on his watch.
He didn't care where I needed to be
and he never played tour guide with me.
He just let my senses catch the prizes
as they shot past.
He knew I'd need those
more than any words
he could fumble to arrange.

Others told me he was a terrible driver.
That's probably true.
I was struck by everything
he drove us through.

THE DAY HE LEFT

I slept through that night.
The morning's tired embers whimpered
as I walked downstairs.
I was told of the fire that didn't wake me
and I concealed the knowledge
of the dry hot tinder
that had waited for a spark.

He'd gone.
Shot out with a pop of intense heat.
He now cooled somewhere in the morning rain,
regretted, reconciled, planned ahead.

And her,
I held her as she shook with denial,
wounded from the burns
but still clenched in readiness.
I asked them to take me to him.
I begged.

The wet streets strobed past
like grey property pages on a printing press.
I wore my hood in the car.
The fur trim tried its best to tickle my red, wet cheeks
but the numbness was defiant.

When we arrived at the house
I kept my hood up as we went inside,
hoping my reveal would be the catalyst
for his reconsideration.
That the sudden face of his son would heal everything.
Such was the ego of a twelve-year-old boy.
He looked at us,
first at his son, then, disappointedly, at his cousin.
This wasn't the time for me.

He made time.

I buried my head in his chest
and gripped him like a cliff face.
He told me he'd always be my dad
but he would now be with her.

I clenched and cried till my eyes swelled.
My tears were a wet snowball hurled at an iceberg,
my pain as searing as a candle to a glacier.
All I had was not enough.

This would not go unpunished.
The betrayal would not be forgotten.
I would not make this an easy victory for them.
They hadn't seen an enemy like me before,
the bullied, artsy, fat boy,
the most underestimated,
unstoppable force they would ever face.
I don't remember the rest of the day.
Just the thrill of the coming fight

which everybody lost.
Kindness won on aggregate.

HE IS HEAVY

Such warmth and density and history.
I am and have always been in his orbit.
Like a satellite trying to be a comet,
desperate to break free and become my own world
just to prove to him I have my own gravity,
my own system.

When I am a planet he is the sun.
When I am the sun he is the centre of the galaxy.
He builds his own gravity so well,
creates energy so simply.

So big and oblivious
his inflections ripple like tremors
through my tectonic plates,
shaking my cities and my bridges,
gouging deep cracks in the landscape,
leaving me to pick up the pieces.

But I won't be outdone.
Not while I exist in his atmosphere.
My weight and my spin pull at his tides.
I have given him such wild storms,
inflicted such damaging tsunamis
just to make him feel me.

I would ignite a supernova
to watch dawn break on his face.
Reorder the cosmos to see
new starlight in his eyes.
Defy physics to show him my will.

Just to make him feel me.
And when his light dims
and his force diminishes
and I finally escape his orbit
I will not collapse into
the black hole he leaves behind.

I will take the pieces he left,
the gravity he built,
the energy he created,
his warmth, history, density,
and I will keep it all spinning
until it finally crashes into me,
strengthening me,
making me heavier.

And those old cracks and broken pieces
will be washed clean by the storms and tsunamis
created by my own satellites
pulling at my tides,
desperate to make me feel them.

THAT'S NICE

In conversation over a Guinness
I confess to a lecturer
that I never want my work to be up its own arse.
He asks what measures I have in place
to detect the location of my output
to ensure it does not take a detour up my rectum.
I tell him I don't want my mother to not get what I'm doing.
He tells me I'm making huge assumptions about
what my mother does and does not 'get'.
'You clearly haven't met my mother,' I say.
I recall all the drawings that have passed
in and out of her hands with a 'that's nice'.
The short films that she left the room
in the middle of.
The myriad stories I've told that were met with
glazed eyes, silence and a swift change of subject.
He winks at me and sips his pint.

Since that evening there have been decades
of doodles, designs, moving images
and adventures written down
which have seldom found their way
under my mother's nose.
Thus, my measurement framework
gathered dust, leaving me no idea
of the position of my work
in relation to my posterior.

But on this day, I climb the stairs of
her house and a cursory glance at the walls
reveals a poster of mine.
In another room, a watercolour.
An ink drawing and three pencil sketches
in the dining room, and in the kitchen
a charcoal drawing and a poem,
and these are good ones, I think.
She makes us a coffee.

I tell her I didn't realise she had so many of
my artworks up on the walls.
She winks at me and sips her coffee,
then swiftly changes the subject.

THE UNINVITED

He'd already made himself at home
when I noticed him sitting there.
I don't know how long he'd been ducking me.
Quietly traipsing around after me.
Incrementally dimming the lights.
Turning off the music.
Hiding messages and invites from friends.
Cooking meals with less and less seasoning
until everything tasted of warm grey.
Telling my son it's too cloudy to go out,
that the rain would ruin everything.
Climbing into bed between me and my wife
and immediately turning out the light,
then whispering into the dark
about all that was missing.

He even followed me to work.
Questioned my every decision, every brushstroke,
every colleague's response,
every meeting I was or wasn't invited to.
He just wanted us to sit together,
wrapped up in a grey, damp tissue blanket.
No warmth, no pain.
Meditating in a dank cupboard
whilst a fidgety old clock ticked nervously
in a dark, boring prefab house falling apart in the rain.

He ached for my company.
He mimicked my voice.
He fooled others into thinking he was me.
He was such a powerful speaker.

But so am I.
As were the voices that called him out
and regaled me of his patterns and methods.
They helped start the eviction process,
though he squatted for months,

pulled every trick to get me to let him stay,
but others need me far more.

I see him in queues now,
in corners, fridges, bookshelves and old threads.
But I talk about him,
warn those I love when his face
sneaks into windows and mirrors.
When I see him sitting on the bed.
When he hands me another bottle.

I can't entertain him.
He's a cousin I have no time for,
a drunk who plays nerves
like a seasoned pianist.
I know he has nowhere else to go
and I know I have the only food he needs
and that he'll always be around.

But so will I,
and I was here first,
and I'm way more fun.

GOD'S DEATHBED

I'm just too old now.
My eyes aren't what they were,
lidded and congealed.
Invisible bones ache
from holding up so many heavens,
feet hot and heavy
from the scorched earth
of burning custody battles.
My mind is weary from pleading voices.
My heart is full of blame.
My voice is drowned.
I'm ready now.
You must let me go.
You will cope.
You have each other.
It's enough.
It always was.

FOR THE LOVE OF DOG

Useless in a meltdown
but everything you need.
Halts your existential crisis
if you take him by the lead.
Doesn't care about your work
or your money or your woes.
Wants your time and your food
and to lick your nose and toes.
He picks up the slack, Jack.
Works with the Prozac.
Gets you out the house
when all you want to do is nap, Jack.
Doesn't give a damn
if you take him with citalopram
or his walking remedies
with the talking therapies.
Self-care? There, there.
Tried prayer. Nothing there.
Hard to miss a fluffy guest
when he needs you, when he's messed.
Such a pest, the very best.
Obsessed.
Not stressed.
Can't offend.
Best friend.
Not coy.
Pure joy.
Fetch toy.

Good boy.

MILLS AND BONE
(ROMANTIC FICTION FOR DOGS)

He was much taller and infinitely more commanding in the flesh than I remembered from our last meeting seventeen minutes ago. He, the salt and pepper-haired master of the house, and I, the lowly but eager head of house security desperate to prove my stock. I couldn't wait to greet him as he strode up the path holding his newspaper, teasing me with it, taunting my canine jaws with this thing I would rip to pieces to show him my power and will. As he approached the door I found my legs shaking with zealous want. Would he remember me? Would it be the same?

I tried to maintain dignity, but within seconds of his key entering the lock I made haste to see him. The sheer majesty of his legs as they entered the hall ignited something inside my loins and I had to have the right one right there and then. I took him by the knee with my front paws and thrust myself upon him again and again. I'm a bad dog, I screamed, such a bad dog. The more I came at him, the more his leg and his body shook. Yes, I said, how I've longed for this. It felt as if our stars were aligning, but without warning he jolted his leg from my grip and took my paws firmly in his hairless grasp. He seemed upset. What had I done? Was this not the right time? Had I overstepped my purview?

It was clear from the cold rigidity in his voice that I had performed an unspeakable indiscretion. I was not worthy of this man, this commander of my heart. I had turned the potential of true love into grubby, base desire. I was on the brink of returning to the basket to tender my letter of resignation when he picked me up in his mighty arms and kissed the top of my head. I melted upon him, licked his chin, nostrils and right ear, and he rubbed me forcefully under my front leg pit, my back leg quivering like a dove's wing. You do love me, I yelped.

The evening crept upon us and we took our constitutional. He graciously let me stop to smell the stale urine and scooped up my ablutions with steadfast dignity and grace. I would serve this man till I died, this distant, powerful, beautiful, hairless man. This lord of the leash was forever to be the owner of my heart. I fetched him one of his slippers as he retired for the night. I'd cheekily dined upon the other one for brunch, but this wasn't the time to tell him. I kissed him on the eyes, nose and left ear and sneaked in a few licks of his toes before retiring to my basket. I could think of nothing else but him as I gently licked my testicles, the light of the moon piercing the curtains and dancing over my fur, stirring in me an ancient, primal power. I howled just a little. He howled back my name. This went on for hours. My heart would never be the same again.

VALENTINIHILIST

Roses are dead.
Violets are too.
Plants never do well in my house.

THIS TREE

Apologies to Joyce Kilmer.

I think that I may never see
a sight more vivid than this tree.
A tree that has given far more than it's got
without ever moving from this spot.
A tree that expresses with leaves it possesses
by mostly creating photosynthesis
which gives breath to poets who study thee
as part of their English Master's degree.
You are magnificent, heavy and clearly old,
brazen, untempered, baffling and bold,
but your most arresting trait by far
is you're currently resting on my car.

WHAT IT IS

It's not being romantic.
It's not being sexy or impressive.
It's not fate or destiny
or anything outside of our control.
It's not providence, divine or infernal.
It's not what you'd expect.

It's being respectful.
It's being attentive, serious and silly.
It's getting out of the way,
it's getting in the way,
it's moving things out of the way.
It's slumping on top of the things
that won't move out of the way
and giggling hysterically with exhaustion.

It's tiring.
It's frustrating.
It's alive and unsafe.
It's a long way down.

It's compromise.
Unchildish compromise that doesn't settle
but finds the gold dust in the tiny patch
of dirt we've been allotted.

It's knowing you know that I'm a
short-tempered, well-meaning idiot
and you knowing I know that you're a
tenacious, subtle, manipulative
megamind with compassion to spare.

It's telling me I'm a fool when I can take it
and letting me fall on my face when I can't.
It's seeing the cracks before the full collapse
and yanking the dam down
and building it back up again.

It's sex when we're tired or ecstatic or lazy
or anxious or shaking, sweaty, drunken messes
and always when we're both ready.
Always that.

It's sailing through oceans of weekdays
clouded with grey duty without words or comfort
and without ever doubting the ship will float,
that the horizon will still want us.

It's ticking off the days to a break without kids
only to spend the day missing them.
That warm joy of missing them together.

It's seeing you hold a battered macabre teddy bear
that will not stay missing despite my best efforts.

It's you watching me replay conversations
in my head that could have gone better
and you knowing exactly which conversations they are.

It's collapsing into bed too tired to even say goodnight
but finding the energy to creak our heads to kiss.

It's watching them wheel you into theatre
not knowing if you're coming out again
and finding the courage to not be me
but that which must endure.
That which stands for as long as it needs to
until we allow it to crumble away to rubble
which we'll build back up again together.

It's knowing, not believing.
It's inevitable, irrefutable, irreducible.
It's what this is.
It's honest love.

Honest, love.

INSPIRATIONAL POEM

On a Monday morning in January
I fasten the buttons on my shirt
and stare out of the window
into the dark of the street.
I absent-mindedly rub my finger
over the last unfastened button
and a deep sigh deflates me.
It's shit out there.

Shit.
And beyond the street and the city
and the clouds and the satellites
shitter still.
Unfathomable, vast, light years of shit
in every direction.
Dangerous shit.
Life-destroying shit.
You need a spacesuit
and an oxygen tank
so you don't die instantly.
It's that shit.

And mostly dark.
Dark and shit.
And massive.
Massive, dark and shit.
And really cold.
Positively brass monkeys

apart from the stars
which are fucking hot.
You're a fritter before you get
within a million miles of them
and there's loads of those buggers everywhere.

And back down here it's a nightmare.
Constantly spinning around

one of those hot, dangerous buggers
while we're pelted at with massive molten rocks
and radiation.
Actual fucking radiation.

And the plumbing down here often buggers up
and we're flooded with filthy, horrible water
with shit in it and we drown or die of disease
or mountains blow up and we fry
or the ground shakes and swallows us up.

And then there's the animals.
Animals with sharp teeth
that eat meat that we're made of.
And there's the tiny ones.
The ones you can't even see.
The ones that kill you from the inside.
You can't even get at those little shits.

And some of the food is actually poisonous.
Food that looks like it's not poisonous
actually is.
And some of it that isn't poisonous to others
will actually kill you.
A bleeding peanut could kill you
or a peanut going down the wrong way
or a tiny bit of peanut in your tea.

And the people in charge
divide the whole place into bits
and tell us which bit we belong to
and what it means to belong to a bit.
Then they get people to fight people from other bits
so they can have more bits
or if they don't agree with one of the people on a bit.
And then they get people to invent ways
to get rid of more and more people

so they can have more and more bits
and the methods get bigger and better
until they can kill everybody with a button.

I fasten my last button.
It really is absolutely fucking incredible
that I'm still here.

And I'm staying.
I've earned it.

ACKNOWLEDGEMENTS

Over the last few years many people have been there for me when I needed them to be. Some have helped me carry loads. Some have let me shuffle in front of their mics to spout my mind and some have been pure inspiration. Behold some thoroughly marvellous people...

FAMILY
Missy, Monkeyface, Curlyfries, Mam, Dad, Sandra, Dave, Babs, Ron, Gem, Russ, Jan, Shmo, Kim, Connor, Claire, Paul, Chris

NORTH EAST
Jeff Price, Kate Fox, Ali Pritchard, Peter Mortimer, Sheila Wakefield, Jenni Pascoe, Steve Urwin, Kirsten Luckins, Rowan McCabe, Matt Abbot, Jason Cook, Steffen Peddie, Ray Laidlaw, Billy Mitchell, Jonathon Wallis, Emma and Graham Onions, Joe Kriss, Donald Jenkins, Phil Rigby, Tony and Jade Gadd, Henry Raby, Stu Freestone, Kate Staines, Ken Brady, Katie Scott, Alfie Joey, Ben Crompton, Simma, Si Beckwith, Joanne Oliver, Beccy Owen, Lindsay Hannon, Ruth Macha

SCOTLAND
Sophia Walker, Jenny Lindsay, Rachel McCrum, Kevin P Gilday, Eleanor Livingstone, Hannah Lavery, MiKo Berry

NORTH WEST
Kieren King, Ella Gainsborough, Ben Mellor, Dave Viney, Richard Duffy, Tony Walsh, Charlie Hart, Mike Garry, Rose Condo, Jackie Hagan, Ciarán Hodgers, Matt Panesh

MIDLANDS
Jess Green, Toby Campion, Bohdan Piasecki, DreadlockAlien, Maggie Doyle, Gemma Baker

SOUTH EAST
Paula Varjack, Dan Simpson, Rob Auton, Dan Cockrill, John Hegley, Laurie Bolger, Steve Larkin, Caroline Teague, Sara Hirsch, Fay Roberts, Neil Spokes, Tina Sederholm, Peter Hunter,

Michael James Parker, Sally Reader, Umor Haque, Jake Wild Hall, Tim Clare, Megan Beech, Joelle Taylor, Salena Godden, Erin Bolens, Hollie McNish

SOUTH WEST

Helen and Benita Johnson (and the Poetry & Words team at Glastonbury), Anna Freeman, Chris Redmond, Clive Birnie, Liv Torc, Robert Garnham, Jon Seagrave, Thommie Gillow, Rebecca Tantony, David Oakwood, Elvis Mcgonagall, AF Harrold, Matt Harvey, Vanessa Kisuule

REST OF THE WORLD

Adrian Timmins, Erin Fornoff, Chelley Brekke McLear

MEDIA

Faith Lawrence and Ian McMillan @ *The Verb* – BBC Radio 3, Phill Jupitus @ BBC Radio 4, BBC Arts, BBC Four, Alan Cumming and Sky Atlantic, BBC Radio Newcastle, Nationwide Building Society and Michael Bolger, Joe McDonnell @ Gumbo Media

There are four quotes in this book that need acknowledging:

In 'She Doesn't Know' the line *'Tell me about the rabbits, George'* is from *Of Mice and Men* by John Steinbeck.

In 'The Right Dreams' the line *'some corner of a foreign field that is forever England'* is from the poem 'The Soldier' by Rupert Brooke.

In 'Prayer for the Selfish' the words *'green and pleasant land'* are from 'Jerusalem' by William Blake.

The button image contains the quote *'Without stories, we wouldn't be human beings at all'* by Philip Pullman.